INDIAN OCEAN TSUNAMI
SURVIVAL STORIES

BY DARICE BAILER

Published by The Child's World®
1980 Lookout Drive • Mankato, MN 56003-1705
800-599-READ • www.childsworld.com

Acknowledgments
The Child's World®: Mary Berendes, Publishing Director
Red Line Editorial: Design, editorial direction, and production
Photographs ©: Eugene Hoshiko/AP Images, cover, 1; Shutterstock Images, 6, 14, 21
(right), 26; A.S. Zain/Shutterstock Images, 8; Dorling Kindersley/Thinkstock, 9; Chaiwat
Subprasom/Reuters/Corbis, 10; Red Line Editorial, 13; Doug Vinez/Shutterstock
Images, 16; Epic Stock Media/Shutterstock Images, 18; Surapan Boonthanom/
Reuters/Corbis, 20; iStockphoto, 21 (left); Mantobing/EPA/Newscom, 22; Harry Page/
Mirrorpix/Newscom, 24; M.A. Pushpa KumaraA/EPA/Corbis, 28

ISBN 9781634074247

LCCN 2015946313

Printed in the United States of America
Mankato, MN
December, 2015
PA02288

ABOUT THE AUTHOR

Darice Bailer wanted to write for children since she was in fifth grade. Today, she is the author of many books for young readers. She enjoys visiting schools and sharing tips about writing with students. She lives with her husband in Connecticut.

TABLE OF
CONTENTS

DISASTER STRIKES

December 26, 2004, was a beautiful morning in Indonesia and other countries along the Indian Ocean. The sun rose in a bright blue sky. The beaches looked like paradise with palm trees and aqua-colored water. But a terrible disaster lurked below.

Just before 8:00 in the morning, one of the largest earthquakes in history rattled the sea off the coast of Indonesia. A piece of ocean floor as big as California shot up 16 feet (5 m). The earth shook for eight to ten minutes. Huge waves rippled in every direction.

The earthquake stunned the people of Indonesia. Some sat in the middle of the street and waited for the ground to stop shaking. In homes, ceilings crashed down. Windows shattered. But the worst was yet to come.

Half an hour later, a tsunami struck Indonesia. A tsunami is a series of giant waves. It can streak through the ocean up to 600 miles per hour (966 km/h)—as fast as a jet. The first tall wave spewed up on shore, like a geyser. Dark-gray, dirty water rushed up the streets and over people. Boats bashed into buildings, and cars and vans swirled around in the water. Houses were washed off the ground and broken into tiny pieces.

The Indian Ocean tsunami struck more than a dozen countries. It is the deadliest tsunami in history. The disaster was a great tragedy. And yet, there were miracles of survival.

FAST FACTS

Date
- Sunday, December 26, 2004

Time
- Earthquake starts at 7:58 a.m.

Known As
- 2004 Indian Ocean tsunami, Christmas tsunami, Boxing Day tsunami

Where It Struck
- Thirteen countries along the Indian Ocean

Size of the Earthquake
- Largest in 40 years

Tallest Wave
- 110 feet (34 m)

Number of People Who Died
- 230,000 estimated

Number of Injuries
- More than 500,000

Cost of Aid and Rebuilding
- $7.5 billion

Chapter 1

RIDING THE WAVE

Wimon Thongtae steered his fishing boat in the Indian Ocean. He was fishing off the coast of Thailand. His boat was long and narrow and looked like it had a tail. A wooden pole stuck out the back. It connected the engine on the boat to a propeller in the water. Thongtae steered the boat by raising and lowering its tail.

Thongtae squinted at shore near where he lived. Something strange was happening. The **tide** was very, very low. Thongtae had never seen so much rocky ocean floor when the tide went out. And this morning, the water around his boat had been clear. Now, the sea was dark and foamy.

Suddenly, a huge wave smacked into Thongtae's boat. The wave lifted the vessel high up before continuing toward shore. The boat crashed down onto the water after the wave passed. Thongtae fell with the boat and landed on the floor with a thud. He heard the boat crack. Fortunately, it was still in one piece.

◄ **Long-tailed fishing boats are common off the coast of southern Thailand.**

▲ **The tsunami destroyed thousands of fishing boats, large and small.**

Thongtae looked around. Other boats were not so lucky. Many splintered apart and **capsized**, dumping their fishermen in the water. Arms **flailed** as men struggled to keep their heads above water.

Looking farther out, Thongtae saw another wave torpedoing toward them. This second wave was black and taller than a telephone pole.

Thongtae thought he was going to die. How could he survive the next wave barreling toward him? Boats tried to drive up onto the wave, but the wave snapped them in half. Thongtae decided his boat might hold up better if it climbed the wave sideways.

Black water pelted him. The boat creaked and wood split, but Thongtae made it to the top of the wave. Then, his boat smashed back down as the wave rolled past. Thongtae hit the floor of the boat headfirst. But he was alive. Of 24 boats in the area, Thongtae's was the only one still whole.

GROWING WAVES

Tsunami waves start to grow taller only as they approach shore. Boats on the open ocean experience a much smaller disturbance than those near land.

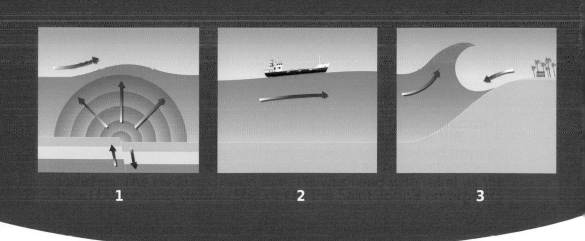

1   2   3

Chapter 2

A TIMELY WARNING

In December 2004, Tilly Smith's family was on vacation. The ten-year-old and her family lived in England. But they were celebrating Christmas at a hotel in Thailand. The morning after Christmas day, Tilly walked on the beach with her family. She felt the tide rush out under her feet on the white sand.

The sea pulled farther and farther away. And on the **horizon**, Tilly saw a white, foamy wave. It looked like froth on top of a glass of soda. Tilly knew something was wrong.

Two weeks earlier, Tilly had learned about tsunamis in school. Her geography teacher showed Tilly's class a video about a tsunami that struck Hawaii in 1946. Tilly had learned that the tide retreats far out before a tsunami. Then, deadly waves rage in.

The same thing was happening now. The ocean had slipped out too far. And the sea was foaming and bubbling.

◄ **Tilly Smith (left) was on vacation with her mother (right) and the rest of her family when the tsunami hit Thailand.**

A tsunami was on its way. Tilly knew big waves were coming in. And there was no time to waste. Everyone needed to get off the beach. There would be only about ten minutes between when the ocean drew back and tsunami waves swept in. If people on the beach did not **evacuate**, they would drown.

Tilly sprung into action. "We must get off the beach, now!" she screamed at her mother, father, and seven-year-old sister.[1] Tilly's mother did not believe her at first. Finally, she followed Tilly back to the hotel. Tilly's father told a security guard that his daughter thought a tsunami was coming.

The security guard ordered everyone off the beach. Tilly ran up the stairs of the hotel with her family. The wind whipped her long blonde hair as she hurried up to the second floor. Then, it hit.

Up on the balcony, Tilly watched huge waves smother the pool, sweep up chairs, and flood the hotel. The water darkened as it bulldozed everything in its way.

There had never been a tsunami like this in Thailand. There was no warning on the beach, except Tilly's. She saved more than 100 people that day.

WHERE IT HAPPENED

The earthquake's epicenter was located off the coast of Indonesia. It took about 90 minutes for the tsunami to reach the southern beaches of Phuket, Thailand, where Tilly Smith and her family were on vacation.

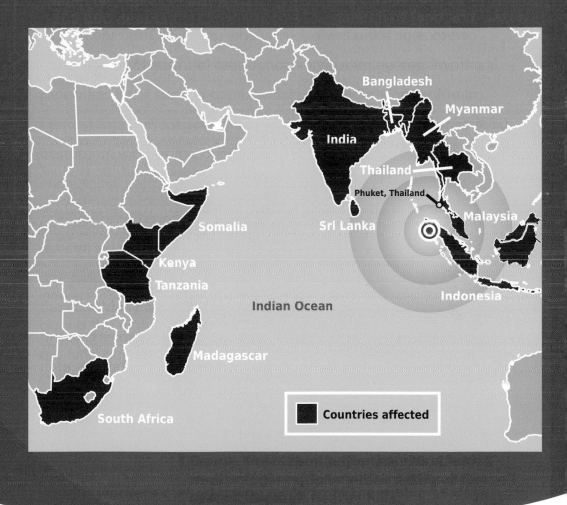

Bangladesh

Myanmar

India

Thailand

Phuket, Thailand

Malaysia

Somalia

Sri Lanka

Kenya

Tanzania

Indonesia

Indian Ocean

Madagascar

South Africa

■ Countries affected

Chapter 3

ANIMAL INSTINCT

As waves struck Thailand, more deadly waves sped west toward the island of Sri Lanka. There is a national park on the island, called Yala. When the first wave reached the island, it would surge through the thick jungle where spotted leopards lived. It would flood the green brush where adult Asian elephants lumbered beside their gray calves. Waves would wash into the jeeps filled with tourists riding down the dirt roads. People come from all over the world to see the park's elephants, leopards, jackals, and crocodiles.

On the day of the tsunami, elephants were walking along the beach. When an elephant senses danger, it makes a sound like a trumpet to warn others. Elephants have sensitive bones in their feet that can feel **seismic vibrations**.

On December 26, 2004, the elephants seemed to know that a killer wave was heading their way. About an hour before the

◄ **An estimated 300 elephants live in Yala National Park.**

▲ **When threatened, elephants use their trunks to make sounds similar to trumpets.**

tsunami, three elephants ran off the beach. One was a young calf. Baby elephants are only 3 feet (1 m) tall. The calf would likely drown if caught in the tsunami.

There were high sand dunes along the beach. On top of the sand dunes, the calf would be safe. The adult elephants trumpeted. The small elephant followed them to the top of a dune. Flamingoes flew up to higher ground, too, away from their low-lying breeding areas.

Finally, people heard the ocean roar that the birds and elephants had anticipated. The noise grew louder and louder.

Then, the sea plowed in. As elephants stood on top of the sand dune, people cried out in different languages. Snakes and lizards had climbed up trees. Soon, people scampered up to join them.

The tsunami waves washed 2 miles (3 km) inland. The water filled buildings with mud and fish. Many people in the park died that day. But somehow, most of the animals in the park survived.

TIMELINE OF THE DISASTER

7:58 a.m.: A massive earthquake shakes the ocean floor.

8:30 a.m.: Huge waves hit the island of Sumatra, Indonesia.

9:30 a.m.: The tsunami strikes southern Thailand.

10:00 a.m.: The tsunami reaches Sri Lanka and India.

2:00 p.m.: The tsunami reaches the eastern coast of Africa.

*All times taken from the time zone where the epicenter of the earthquake occurred.

Chapter 4

CAUGHT IN THE RUSH

Karin Svard watched her husband and three boys play on the beach the morning of the tsunami. The family lived in Sweden, but they were spending the Christmas holiday in Thailand. The Svard boys were ages 10, 11, and 14.

Svard noticed something strange was happening that day. The tide rushed out so fast that fish could not keep up. Helpless, the colorful fish flopped in the sand. Then, Svard saw the white wave out on the ocean. It zoomed closer, like a speeding train. The first wave neared the beach and slowed down. The tsunami waves behind it bunched up to form a white wall of water.

When Svard saw the towering wave, her eyes widened and her heart pounded with fear. Svard screamed at her children. "Look at the wave! Look at the wave!"[2] She ran to her boys, desperate to save them. But Svard's husband and boys disappeared in the

◀ **As tsunamis approach shore, they begin to break, or crash down.**

▲ **Southern Thailand is a common tourist attraction. More than 500 Swedish citizens died in the tsunami.**

torrent of white foamy water. The wave yanked Svard under, too. She swallowed sandy water, mud, and pine needles.

The wave swept Svard and **debris** inland. If only she could find something to hold on to in the middle of this ocean tornado. Svard saw a palm tree and grabbed on to a branch. She climbed the trunk and held on. Then, she watched the first wave rush back and out to sea. If she had been in the water, she would have been dragged along with it.

The first tsunami wave had passed. But it was not the most dangerous one. Up in the tree, Svard watched a second wave charge inland. This time, the wave was so tall it washed over her head. Where was the top of the water? Where could she breathe? Pool chairs whipped into her. Svard thought she was going to die. How would her husband and sons survive the monster wave?

Finally, ten minutes later, the tsunami was over. Looking around, Svard found her husband and her three boys. They, too, had held on to trees in the giant waves. Now, they hugged each other, grateful to be alive.

HEIGHT OF THE WAVE

By the time the tsunami reached shore, it had a maximum height of 110 feet (34 m). That is about 10 times taller than an average school bus.

Chapter 5

WAKING UP STRANDED

The morning of the tsunami, eight-year-old Martunis was playing soccer with his friends in his hometown of Banda Aceh, Sumatra. Martunis felt the earth rumble. Then, he saw a big wave coming. He quickly jumped in the family car with his family. Martunis's mother tried to drive them to a safe place. But the road in front of them was blocked with cars and bikes. Everyone was trying to escape. "The sea is rising!" people screamed.[3]

The ocean grew louder and louder. It was right behind them. Soon, dark water washed over Martunis's feet and legs and rose in the car. The water kept getting higher and higher. Then, it hoisted the car and flipped it over and over again. Martunis smacked his head on the side of the car. Then, he blacked out.

Martunis woke up and found himself floating in the ocean. When the tsunami rushed back out to sea, it must have swept him

◀ **Martunis was wearing the jersey of his favorite soccer star when the tsunami struck.**

▲ **The coast of Sumatra was littered with trash after the tsunami.**

with it. It was a miracle Martunis had not drowned. The water around Martunis was filled with garbage. There was broken wood, twisted metal, and telephone poles. The ocean looked like a trash dump.

Martunis had no idea where he was. He saw a school chair floating beside him and grabbed it. When he found a mattress, he climbed on. Waves took him to a swampy area. Martunis had no idea where he was, and he could not swim. He stayed afloat.

Martunis was hungry, so he hunted around in the trash. He found bottles of water and packets of noodles. He fished them out of the water and stored them on his mattress.

Nineteen days later, Martunis had eaten everything around the mattress. All his food and water were gone.

After two more days, rescuers found Martunis. A crew drove him to the hospital. Martunis learned that his mother and brothers did not survive the tsunami. But Martunis's father and grandmother found him at the hospital and stayed by his bed.

BIGGEST EARTHQUAKES SINCE 1900

The Indian Ocean tsunami was the third largest since 1900. Hundreds of aftershocks occurred in the following weeks.

Location	Date	Magnitude	Number of Deaths
Chile	May 22, 1960	9.5	1,655
Alaska	March 28, 1964	9.2	131
Indian Ocean	December 26, 2004	9.1	230,000
Japan	March 11, 2011	9.0	15,703
Russia	November 4, 1952	9.0	0

Chapter 6

HIGH AND DRY

Two days after the tsunami, policemen found a young boy shivering in a tree in Thailand. The little boy was only three years old. His name was Wathanyu Silao, but his nickname was Diew.

When the wave lashed onto shore, Diew's mother held him and tried to run away as fast as she could. Diew wrapped his arms tightly around his mother. He looked back and saw the huge wave chasing them. A tsunami wave can race onto shore as fast as 100 miles per hour (161 km/h).

Soon, the wave caught up to and washed over both of them. Diew and his mother could not hold on to each other. The ocean ripped him out of his mother's arms. Diew could not see anything in the murky water. It lifted him up and swept him along. He was not strong enough to fight the powerful wave.

◀ **Signs near the coast in Thailand tell people where to go if a tsunami approaches.**

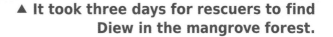

▲ It took three days for rescuers to find Diew in the mangrove forest.

The tsunami carried Diew into a forest of **mangrove** trees. Up in the trees, Diew grabbed a branch to climb. He was safe in the treetops. But he could not get down to find his mother.

Diew was alone in the forest. Night fell and mosquitoes buzzed around him. They bit him in the dark, and Diew was scared. There was a chance he could fall out of the tree when he slept. And he was hungry. There was nothing for him to eat or drink.

Finally, on the third day, Diew heard the sound of helicopters. He looked up to see one whirring above him. But the men in the helicopter could not see him in the treetops.

Then, Diew heard men in boats approaching. They were police officers. Diew cried out to let them know he was there.

The men gave Diew some water to drink and drove him to the hospital.

Eventually, Diew's mother found him at the hospital. When she did, she could not stop kissing her son and crying out, "It's a miracle!"[4]

HARDEST-HIT COUNTRIES

The Indian Ocean tsunami killed more than 230,000 people and left millions homeless. The country nearest the epicenter of the earthquake, Indonesia, was the hardest hit.

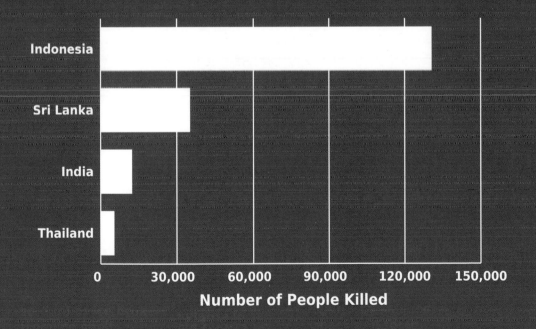

GLOSSARY

capsized (KAP-sized): When a boat is capsized, it has turned over in the water. Many long-tail boats capsized during the tsunami.

debris (duh-BREE): Debris contains pieces of wreckage or broken things. The tsunami caused so much damage that countries were littered with debris.

evacuate (i-VAK-yoo-ate): To evacuate is to move away from a dangerous area. There was no warning before the tsunami to allow people to evacuate safely.

flailed (flaled): A person who has thrashed his or her arms or legs wildly has flailed. People flailed in the water, struggling to stay afloat.

horizon (huh-RYE-zun): The horizon is where the sky and earth or sea seem to meet. Many people saw something strange on the horizon before the big waves rolled in.

mangrove (man-GROVE): A mangrove is a tropical tree or shrub that grows in marshes or tidal shores. The little boy hid in the top of the mangrove tree until he was rescued.

seismic vibrations (SIZE-mik vi-BRAY-shunz): Seismic vibrations are when the ground trembles from an earthquake. Elephants can feel seismic vibrations through their feet.

tide (tide): Tide is the rise and fall of the ocean's surface that occurs because of the pull of the sun and moon on the earth. Right before the tsunami, people watched the tide slip far out to sea.

torrent (TOR-ent): A torrent is a violent stream of liquid. The massive earthquake sent a torrent of waves speeding across the ocean.

SOURCE NOTES

1. "10 Year Old Girl Saves Dozens from Tsunami." *The Sun*. News Group Newspapers Ltd., 1 Jan. 2005. Web. 25 Jun. 2015.

2. Andy Lines. "Mum was Screaming: Look at the Wave!" *The Mirror Online*. MGN Ltd., 3 Jan. 2005. Web. 25 Jun. 2015.

3. Dan Rivers. "Tsunami Survivor: Baby Brought Me Luck." *CNN.com*. Turner Broadcasting System, Inc., 23 Dec. 2009. Web. 25 Jun. 2015.

4. "Mother and Child Reunited." *The Nation*. Nation Multimedia, 30 Dec. 2004. Web. 25 Jun. 2015.

TO LEARN MORE

Books

Fine, Jil. *Tsunamis*. New York: Children's Press, 2007.

Fradin, Judy, and Dennis Fradin. *Tsunamis: Witness to Disaster*. Washington, DC: National Geographic, 2008.

Stiefel, Chana. *Tsunamis*. New York: Scholastic, 2009.

Walker, Niki. *Tsunami Alert!* New York: Crabtree Publishing, 2006.

Web Sites

Visit our Web site for links about the Indian Ocean tsunami: childsworld.com/links

Note to Parents, Teachers, and Librarians: We routinely verify our Web links to make sure they are safe and active sites. So encourage your readers to check them out!

INDEX